LILLE!
D R A

Interactive Dinner Theatre for Outreach

by

Dave Avanzino
Coley Fisher
Craig Wilson

Lillenas PUBLISHING COMPANY

KANSAS CITY, MO 64141

Uncle Phil's Diner
Copyright © 2000 by Dave Avanzino, Coley Fisher, Craig Wilson

This is a royalty play. Permission to perform this work is granted when a Production Pack containing scripts for the cast and director is purchased and the royalty is paid two weeks prior to the performance(s). The performance licensing fee for this play is $35.00 for the first performance and $25.00 for each subsequent performance. Please use the form in the back of this book to register your performance(s) and to submit the royalty payment. You may make copies of the form or submit the information in the form of a letter.

The following should appear in your printed program:
    "Produced by special arrangement with Lillenas Publishing Co."

Lillenas Publishing Company
P.O. Box 419527
Kansas City, MO 64141
Phone: 816-931-1900; Fax: 816-412-8390
E-mail: drama@lillenas.com
Web: www.lillenasdrama.com

Printed in the United States.

PLEASE NOTE: Songs that are suggested for use in this script are only suggestions. It is the responsibility of the performer(s) to obtain any permission necessary to use such songs. Lillenas Publishing Co. is not responsible for any fees when such permission is obtained, nor any damages if permission is not obtained and songs are used illegally.

Cover art by Dave Avanzino & Michael Walsh

Dedication

To the God of all creation
who shares His creativity with us
and gives us the unique ability
to create art, music, and theatre to His glory.

Contents

Acknowledgments   7

Production Notes   9

    An Evening of Interactive Theatre, Food, and Music   9

    Uncle Phil's Diner Outline   10

    Cast   11

    Rehearsing   13

    Food and Service Suggestions   14

    Ticket Sales   15

    Seating   16

    Costuming   17

    Technical   17

    Lighting   18

    Creative Leadership Team   18

    Set Design and Decor   20

    Prop List   25

Uncle Phil's Diner   27

Appendixes   47

    Time Line   47

    Individual Event Descriptions   49

    Cast Descriptions   53

    Bingo Calls   63

Performance Licensing Agreement   64

Acknowledgments

We would like to thank all the incredible people at University Praise in Fullerton, California, for helping to bring the original *Uncle Phil's Diner* to life. One day I was asked by our worship leader, Tamila Zahrndt, if I had any ideas for an outreach event. I told her that I've had an idea for a few years to do this wild, interactive '50s-themed dinner theatre event. She graciously gave me the go-ahead, and I was fortunate to have two incredibly talented people help me flesh it out—Coley Fisher and Craig Wilson. Creating and rehearsing a show that uses a lot of improvisation is not easy, but we had a great cast who worked very hard and gave it their all. None of us was really sure how well it would work right up until the moment we opened the doors. What followed were two of the most exciting and enjoyable evenings I've ever been a part of. People are still talking about it, a year and a half later, and wondering where the sequel is.

One of the reasons it was so successful was that our congregation jumped on board with our vision of outreach. These evenings were not meant to be entertainment for our Body. They were designed to introduce people to who we are through this unique event. Our desire was to communicate our love for God through the talents and creativity He has blessed us with. The cast worked hard, but it was only because of the work of our congregation that almost half of our guests each night were visitors.

Thanks also to Paul Miller and Kim Messer at Lillenas, who gave us the opportunity to share this work with others to the glory of God.

We sincerely hope you will have as wonderful an experience performing *Uncle Phil's Diner* as we did and that it will be a blessing to your group as well as to the people who attend your event.

Dave Avanzino

Production Notes

An Evening of Interactive Theatre, Food, and Music

The goal behind *Uncle Phil's Diner* is to create a warm, fun, and welcoming environment for the members of your church or group to bring their friends and family to. It is an unusual collection of improv, music, choreography, sketch comedy, and food. While there is a definite stage area, the hope is that this event will happen all around the guests, including them as often as possible, making them feel a part of it and not just as observers. A visit to Uncle Phil's is not a passive experience. While there are specific, scripted events throughout the evening, much of the entertainment comes from the '50s-era wait staff interacting and improvising with the guests. They often recognize Uncle Bob or their science teacher Mr. Kroeger sitting at their table and catch up on school and family stories. They interact with one another in small skits and bits designed to amuse people. They occasionally join in on choreographed production numbers. They also *actually* serve food and drinks to the guests. This isn't always necessary but makes for a real "diner" feel. A simple menu of hamburgers, french fries, and Cokes is all you need. This can be prepared easily and inexpensively by you, or you can have it catered. For dessert you can serve chocolate shakes, Oreos, and coffee. Each actor/server is assigned certain tables he or she will be responsible for, just like a real diner. The evening is designed to run for approximately one and a half to two hours. Most of the food should be served in the first hour. After that, more of the audience's attention will be directed to the front. As designed, there is only a short and simple message in the production. The goal is to make people feel welcome and show them how we express our love for God through our creativity and hospitality. This is specifically an outreach event, and church members should be encouraged to invite other people. An important goal would be to make the rest of your congregation feel like they are a part of this event. This should be more than just an evening of entertainment for the congregation. It should be approached as a bridge-building event with the community. You can include information about your church on the menus as well as have information/mailing list cards on the tables for people to fill out. You can also hand them a card as they exit, thanking them for visiting and inviting them back. For that last '50s touch, add a Tootsie Roll!

Uncle Phil's Diner Outline

The setting is 1956 in a small diner in "Your town," U.S.A. The waiters and waitresses in the diner are a strange collection of kids from the town, including a number of high school bobby-soxers, jocks, nerds, cheerleaders, and others. They do their best to engage the guests in conversation, and often entertain them with their antics and interactions with each other. Occasionally they jump up onstage or in the aisles and perform choreographed production numbers to the songs playing. Uncle Phil is a slightly crusty and nervous man in his early 50s. He is trying to find ways to increase business in his diner, so he has lined up a band to come and play tonight—The Desotos. The problem is, they never make it. The band is from the next town over, Herdville, and the leader, Jimmy, forgot to bring the directions when they left. Jimmy has no sense of direction and often gets lost even going home from school. Throughout the evening, Uncle Phil repeatedly gets phone calls updating him on the band's progress in trying to locate the diner. Needless to say, Uncle Phil is a little uptight at this point. He becomes more agitated after each phone call and is terrified that everyone will leave if the band doesn't show up. So he does whatever he can to fill the time. Helping him is his nephew, Phil (called Phil "Jr." to distinguish him from his uncle), who fancies himself a disc jockey who goes by the name P. J.—"P. J. the deejay." He "spins platters" from the stage to give the room some atmosphere and is the emcee for the evening. P. J. is the one who lined up the band for his uncle, so he feels a little responsible. Also helping Uncle Phil is Flodene, the senior waitress. Flodene has seen it all and is everyone's "mom." Among the various distractions they come up with are a bubble gum blowing contest, "This Was Your Life," a nerd love song, and other activities designed to take the audience's attention off the fact that the band hasn't shown up. Uncle Phil's mother keeps pestering him to let her play bingo with everyone. He finally lets her, and it turns out that everyone in the room gets "Bingo" at the same time. This presents a problem for Mom, who only has one prize. She runs. Finally, at the end of his rope, Uncle Phil asks Flodene about the instruments stacked up in the corner. She informs him they belong to the guys in the kitchen who practice after hours. He asks if they're any good. "That's debatable," she says, but he drags them out and makes them play. Flodene forces various members of the wait staff to do some numbers in groups or as solos. The band plays for about a half hour and Uncle Phil, relieved at last, has a short talk with Flodene, where he explains why he feels called to keep hiring so many kids to work for him. He tells her about the man that took a chance on him when he was young and turned him from what could have been a very troubled life. He finally thanks everyone for coming and lets the band play on.

Cast

It is recommended that you have two to three types of casts in this production: Cast A, Cast B, and Cast C. The wait staff at Uncle Phil's is supposed to be in high school, but you may want to cast it with college age and young adult people playing younger. The main reason for this suggestion is that this event requires a lot from your actors. They need to be able to improvise, stay in character, act, serve food, and be prepared for anything that might come up. You need to be able to trust them to know what is funny, as well as what is not funny, as you let them loose in the room. If you have really talented high schoolers who can handle the amount of improv and confidence necessary, go for it. Uncle Phil, Flodene, and Mom should be older adults if possible.

Cast A includes the main characters who move the story line forward (Uncle Phil, P. J., Mom, and Flodene) as well as your main group of wait staff who improv with the guests. The number of wait staff can vary depending on the number of tables you set up and how many people you expect. It is recommended that each main wait staff is assigned only from one to three tables of guests, so cast accordingly. Cast A (except Phil and Mom) will learn all of the production numbers and be "onstage" for the entire evening.

Each member of Cast A will need to select or be assigned a character to portray throughout the evening. They will be in costume and in character the entire time. They will need to develop their characters and how they are going to improv/interact with both the guests as well as the other cast members. Cast A is designed to provide much of the entertainment during the evening. They are who people will remember, so they need to be able to improvise well with the guests.

Most of the characters listed in Cast A don't require specific singing abilities, but a couple of them do. These include:

- Tammy—sings a sad love song such as "Tammy"
- Wally—sings a rock classic such as "Johnny Be Good"
- P. J.—sings a rock and roll standard such as "Great Balls of Fire"

The other songs can be sung by any of the other cast members. Remember, people have come to know these characters throughout the evening, and the more you can play off that during the musical portion, the better.

Cast B is another group of characters, in costume, who are there mainly to assist Cast A in serving their tables. A member of Cast B is assigned to each member of Cast A as a kind of "busperson" to help get the food out faster, to take over if the Cast A member suddenly has to run onstage for something, and to help clear the tables later. This group has a much lower commitment level and can even be different from night to night. They need to be in costume but don't need to learn choreography, and so forth. You can use your high school group or different Bible school classes each night.

Cast C are the members of the band. This production really needs to have a live band. The ongoing gag is that the Desotos never show up, so there needs to be some playoff at the end. The kitchen band is not seen until the last segment of the show. When Uncle Phil has finally given up on the Desotos showing up, Flodene drags these guys out of the kitchen to play. They enter from the kitchen wearing aprons and paper hats, set up their instruments, and then play. If they are also capable of singing a song or two, let them. However, they don't need to be actors. This can be a very small group. At a minimum you would need drums, keyboard, bass, and electric guitar. You can add to that if you want. If you do not have adequate players in your congregation, consider recruiting from your community, other churches, local schools, and colleges. This may be a great opportunity to get some new people involved.

Rehearsing

This is a difficult type of piece to rehearse since many of the elements require a live audience to play off of. What is suggested is that you get the Cast A members together several times to talk through their characters and what they will say to the guests at their tables as well as work up bits of business with one another. For example, Wally can practice asking all of the girls for a date and they can work up their excuses for avoiding it. Ritchie can practice trying to convince other cast members to vote for him for class president by explaining his platform and then debating with them. You can have separate rehearsals for the main cast of Phil, P. J., Mom, and Flodene who have actual lines to memorize and practice. You can also have separate musical and choreography rehearsals. As you get closer to the event, bring these elements together and walk through the show with Cast A. Set up a room with chairs to represent the number of tables you will have the night of your event. Assign cast members their tables and begin practicing moving around in character and interacting with each other. If possible, bring in some of the members of Cast B to act as guests who can be used in the game shows and skits. Be sure to rehearse *all* of the audience participation pieces with people, including the bubble gum contest, "This Was Your Life," and the "Happy Birthday" bit. Your cast needs to see how these work with people to figure how best to do them. The goal is for the cast to become familiar with the series of events for the evening. You will never know exactly what it will be like until you get guests in the room, so the more familiar everyone is with the order of the show, the easier it will go. It is recommended that you bring in all of your Cast B for your final rehearsal so they will also have some idea of what to expect. Your rehearsals will generally be much shorter than the actual performances, so don't worry.

• **NOTE on appropriate improvisation**. The main reason for getting together and practicing the casts' improvs together is to determine if there are certain things that might be inappropriate to use. A lot of things that might seem funny can be insulting or offensive to people. Put-downs or making fun of each other can be funny but can also be viewed as mean. Just be aware of what you are saying, and remember who your audience is.

• **NOTE on selecting audience members**. A couple of the events during the evening require an individual to be selected from the audience. These events are "Happy Birthday" and "This Was Your Life." Both of these events, while very funny, could potentially upset the person. It is suggested that each night you have all of your wait staff "scout" their tables for the right person. They can give their suggestions to the director who will pass on the final selection to P. J. It is always fun, and safer, to use people you know from your group, but it can be more rewarding to pick someone you know is a visitor. If you do this, make sure you know who brought the visitor and pull him or her aside and see how he or she thinks the person would respond. NEVER put someone up front who you know will not like it. This will take away from the intended humor of the event, but more importantly, it will make that person leave with bad feelings.

• **NOTE**. Remind the cast and crew that the fact that the Desotos never show up is a *secret* that they need to keep from their friends and guests. That is the main gag of the evening; and if people know that coming in, it will be less entertaining.

Food and Service Suggestions

Since you are trying to re-create a diner, go for diner food in a diner setting. A simple menu of hamburgers and/or hot dogs, french fries, and sodas is all you need. Limiting the menu makes your job easier. Giving people too many choices complicates your job immensely. There will always be someone who doesn't like what you serve, but you can't help that. Remember, the food is only one element of the evening. Hopefully the entire evening will be so memorable that any shortcomings in the food will be forgotten. Obviously, you can get more elaborate if your budget and facilities allow. One way to involve more people from your congregation would be to line up a Bible school class or other group to handle all the food preparation. This would take a great burden off the cast and would make it more of a churchwide event.

Another suggestion is to have someone come in and cater the event. Shop around and see what kind of deal you can get. Handing this element over to an outside source may be worth it compared to doing it yourselves.

Each Cast A member should be assigned one to three tables depending on the number of tables you set up. They will be responsible for taking the orders and serving the food to their tables as well as keeping up with the evening's activities. To help them, assign a member of Cast B to assist.

It is best to get the main food out of the way early, then focus more on the entertainment. As guests are seated they are handed a menu, and within 15 minutes their order is taken and their drinks are served. Getting the meal out of the way within the first hour is preferable because while people are eating, it is hard for them to focus their attention away from the table. This is the time your wait staff spends interacting with the guests and each other throughout the room. Later in the evening you can serve dessert. Make sure you have enough drinks to be able to give refills throughout the evening.

You can use round or rectangular tables, but you will need to leave space enough for people to walk through easily and, at times, even dance. Don't overcrowd the room for the sake of getting more people in. It will make the type of entertainment going on more difficult.

If you decide a full meal is too much trouble or expense, do a dessert. You can serve ice cream sundaes, banana splits, Oreos, chocolate shakes, and so forth. You will need to determine where in the evening you wish to do this. If you are only serving dessert, wait a little while before doing so. You can start off with serving coffee and drinks, and bring out the food later in the evening.

Ticket Sales

If it is possible to do this event without charging, go for it. This will make a great impression on your guests. For most of us, this is not possible. This is just a suggestion, but if you need to charge, sell tickets as opposed to having an offering. Visitors expect an offering, and one of the goals of an event like this is to show them the unexpected. In selling tickets, target your congregation to purchase them for their guests. Explain your goals and your needs, and get the congregation on board with your vision. If you can accurately convey your vision, people will more than likely get excited about it with you. One idea is to sell the guest tickets for half the price of the member tickets. This helps cover your costs and helps them become part of it with you. You can either have assigned seating or not. Assigned seats can speed up actual seating, but it does take more time and effort to organize. Try to sell as many "presale" tickets as possible. You will always have walk-ins, but it is easier if you know exactly how many people to plan for, especially when food is involved. Offer an incentive for people to plan ahead by charging more at the door for tickets than you do presale tickets. You may want to set aside a certain number of tickets for each night specifically for walk-ins. It can leave a bad impression if people get turned away at the door.

Another idea to encourage your group to bring guests is to offer a discount for guest tickets. The price of a ticket for a guest can be half of the price for a ticket for a member. This is also a great way to keep track of how many visitors you have each night and can be a great incentive for people to invite their friends.

Seating

The goal is to get people seated as quickly as possible. You can use a lot of your Cast B people to help speed this up. The evening's events can start as soon as a large number of the audience is seated. Wait until you have several people waiting to come in before you begin seating. Have a couple of people taking tickets, and Hazel, the main hostess, greeting and assigning tables from a floor plan. The tables need to have numbers and as she gives the guests a table number, a cast member can take them to their seats. Hazel can cross out those seats on her floor plan. Start in the middle of your room and work outward. The atmosphere of the event needs to begin from the moment your guests are in line to come in. You can have cast members walking around outside talking with them or talking to each other in front of them. Another suggestion is to find someone who has classic cars and would be willing to park them in front. Make sure there is music playing from the very beginning. (See Suggested Floor Plan page 22.)

A couple of suggestions regarding room setup: First of all, don't overcrowd your tables. You will need adequate room for the servers to move easily through the room for food service and for several of the evening's events. You also want your guests to feel comfortable, and squeezing too many people in won't help accomplish this. There are also safety and fire code issues to be aware of. Another thing to consider is the placement of your stage area. If you have a long room with a stage at one end, you might consider putting the stage area along the side wall instead of at the end. This makes it easier to see from most of the tables and keeps it at more of an audience level, making your guests feel more a part of it. (See Set Suggestions, page 20.)

Costuming

Costuming for Uncle Phil's is relatively easy. However, remember you are trying to re-create 1956 as much as possible. A lot of the Cast A characters' personalities are expressed through their clothing, so it is recommended that you don't have everyone in any kind of diner uniform. Instead, make up "Uncle Phil's" buttons and name badges that will unify them. There are plenty of books on the '50s that you can find for period costume suggestions. You can also rent movies set in the '50s for costume reference. Your Cast B members can wear something as simple as jeans and a white T-shirt for the guys, and a skirt, blouse, and sweater for the girls. Hair can also help define the era, so be sure to look for references on this also.

Technical

This production uses suggested music as well as sound effects, occasional live music, and roving actors. You will need to determine what will work best for you in setting this up. A minimum of four wireless mikes should be used. The more you have, the easier it is, but you can make do with only a few. The general wait staff doesn't need microphones. Their improv only needs to be heard by their immediate tables. If it needs to be louder, they can yell. P. J. always has one on (or he could use a handheld mike all the time), Flodene, Uncle Phil, and Mom have them but can switch them with other actors occasionally. For the "This Was Your Life" skit, each actor will need to enter with a mike on. These can be traded off with another actor each time the actor leaves stage. A backstage mike is also needed for this skit. Four mikes on stands will be needed for the live music portion of the evening.

A big consideration is how you will run the evening's recorded music. There should *always* be music playing in the background whenever there is no specific action onstage. From the moment people step into the room, there needs to be music. This really sets the mood and period and carries it throughout the evening. If it is possible for P. J. himself to do it from his booth on the stage, this would be preferable. He is one of the main people who stops and starts the series of events during the evening, and the more control over the music he has the better. It is recommended to prerecord a few hours' worth of '50s music on minidisc for playing. This gives a larger variety to pick from and is very flexible. It can also be run from CDs or tapes.

You will need a second sound booth somewhere else in the room to handle the mikes, and the band and vocalists later. The recorded music can be run from here if necessary. The sound effect of the phone ringing is also played from this booth.

Lighting

There is very little specialty lighting for this production. You will need overall, preferably dimmable, room lighting for your guests to see what they are eating and some focused lighting on your stage area. As the evening goes along it may get more and more difficult to get everyone's attention to the stage. You can always dim the room lighting at certain points to get their attention focused where you want it. It is recommended that you have two spotlights. These are used in the "Nerds in Love"* duet and can also be used in "This Was Your Life" and with the music at the end. The "Nerds in Love"* duet is supposed to be a dream sequence, so it is recommended that when this begins, the house lights go out, the spots hit the two actors and follow them through the song. When it ends, the house lights come back up and everyone goes on like nothing happened. Besides that, you can go as simple or as elaborate as you want.

*Sheet music included in Production Pack MPK-825. Call 1-800-877-0700 or visit a local Christian bookstore to order.

Creative Leadership Team

As with any type of production, the more organized you are and the more people you can get involved, the better. This event is designed to be an outreach to your community and is best accomplished if it becomes more of a churchwide project rather than just a music or drama department project. There are many areas in which a variety of people can get involved and take charge of outside the performance areas. This gives a great opportunity for different members of your church to partner together in this outreach.

The main positions you need to consider*:

- PRODUCER
- DIRECTOR
- MUSICAL DIRECTOR
- TECHNICAL DIRECTOR
- CHOREOGRAPHER
- SETS AND ROOM DECOR COORDINATOR
- FOOD PRODUCTION COORDINATOR
- MINISTRY COORDINATOR
- ADVERTISING COORDINATOR

---

*Some of these positions can be combined.

PRODUCER: The producer is responsible for making sure everyone else gets his or her job done and tries to make the event run smoothly and pleasantly for all involved. He or she oversees all the elements of the production (i.e., room reservation, food preparation, rehearsal schedules, and personnel involvement). This requires a detail-oriented person who is a good motivator and encourager.

DIRECTOR: The director is mainly responsible for the cast and the shape and direction the show will take. He or she may be directly involved in other areas like the set, lighting, and so forth. During the show, it is recommended that the director be "onstage" in costume (not responsible for serving any tables). He or she can move through the room and communicate with both P. J. and the sound techs to cue each new event. This is needed to keep the evening moving along at a good pace.

MUSICAL DIRECTOR: The musical director rehearses the actors on their specific songs as well as assembling and working with the band.

TECHNICAL DIRECTOR/LIGHTS AND SOUND: Responsible for arranging all technical elements for the evening, including lighting and sound system. Also needs to arrange for crew to run lights and sound.

CHOREOGRAPHER: Teaches the cast the production numbers as outlined in the script.

SETS AND ROOM DECOR COORDINATOR: Responsible for designing and building sets for the evening as well as dressing the room and tabletops. Also responsible for overseeing the striking of the set when done.

FOOD PRODUCTION COORDINATOR: Responsible for preparing and/or providing for all the food to be served. This could be taken over by a Bible school class, men's group, or so forth.

MINISTRY COORDINATOR: Responsible for all the personnel working the event other than the cast members. This is the person who works to recruit setup and tear-down crews, clean up, kitchen help, food preparation, and so forth. One suggestion is to get different Bible school classes to volunteer to adopt a night to work the event or adopt a night when they will commit to bringing a guest.

ADVERTISING: This is important if you hope to get visitors. The best way to get them, however, is if your members invite them. Work on ways to advertise to your church "why" you are doing this event and get them onboard with your vision. You can even print up a '50s-style invitation they can hand out to their friends. Many local papers and radio stations have free listings for events like these that you may be able to take advantage of also.

Set Design and Decor

This production requires little or even no set to work. You can simply decorate the existing walls of your room, or you can build a small set consisting of a few flats. (See Set Design Illustration, page 23.) It is best to get the stage area up off the floor a little—about 2' is best. Your guests will be sitting, but by raising the stage a little, you will improve the sight lines and make the action onstage more visible. If the stage gets too high, the audience may feel more removed from the action and less a part of it.

If you build flats, one idea is to incorporate a swinging door that would lead offstage into the "kitchen." This is how Uncle Phil and his mom would enter the stage, but not the wait staff. You can also have a door that doesn't open, just for the look of it. If everyone just enters from the side of the stage, it will be fine also. The walls can be painted with a black and white tile pattern 3' up and a pink or seafoam green above that. A molding trim across the seam and along the top edge in a third color (dark pink, silver) will finish off the flats. Using real moldings and door trim will add to the look of the set. The walls can be decorated with posters, "Uncle Phil's" logo (both included in the Production Pack MPK-825*) movie posters from the '50s, soda signs (like Coca-Cola) and even old records. These same themes can be continued around the rest of the room and tables. A main prop for the stage is a phone. A pay phone mounted to the wall is recommended, but a regular old phone can be sitting on the deejay station. Other items that can dress the stage are chrome stools and even a real jukebox if you can find one. Many companies will rent these.

P. J.'s deejay booth should be on the stage. This can be any kind of cart or table that has his sound equipment on it. If you are going to use modern equipment like CD or minidisc players, shield them from the audience. Find an old record player and some old albums in the covers, and cover his booth with them.

For the tables, simple tablecloths and place mats can dress them up. In the center you can put ketchup and mustard dispensers, salt and pepper shakers, and other condiments. If you are going to seat people by table numbers, you will need to have some identification on the tables. An old 45 record on a table stand with a number on it works well and fits the theme.

Remember, this is supposed to *be* 1956, not just look like it. Try to avoid using decor that says things like, "The Fabulous '50s." They would not have had that up back then.

The poster artwork and Uncle Phil's logos (included in the Production Pack MPK-825*) can be enlarged at many copying stores or blueprint businesses. Some 18" x 24" copiers will even take your own paper. You can buy colored art papers at an art store and then enlarge the designs onto them. These can then be painted or colored to add more impact. Blueprint copiers can go up to 4' wide by any length, but usually only onto white paper. The Uncle Phil's logos can be enlarged on these and then spray-mounted onto cardboard, cut out, and hung on the walls or even out in front.

---

*Call 1-800-877-0700 or visit a local Christian bookstore to order Production Pack MPK-825.

Suggested Room Layout

Stage is centered along side wall of room rather than at one end. This allows the audience to be more a part of the action rather than removed from it. Keeping the stage low (2') helps this also.

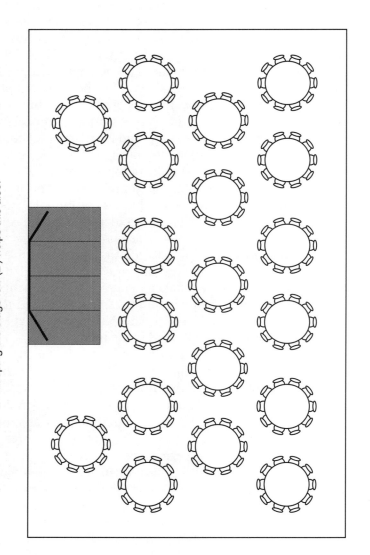

Stage Flat Suggestion

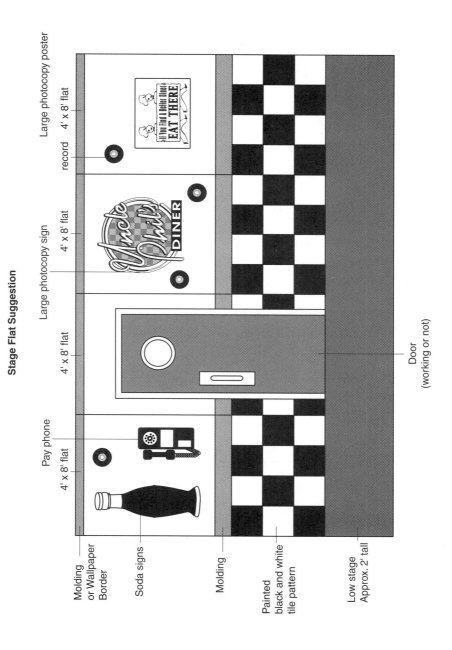

Large photocopy poster

record — 4' x 8' flat

Large photocopy sign — 4' x 8' flat

4' x 8' flat

Pay phone

4' x 8' flat

If You Find A Better Diner EAT THERE

Uncle Phil's DINER

Door
(working or not)

Molding
or Wallpaper
Border

Soda signs

Molding

Painted
black and white
tile pattern

Low stage
Approx. 2' tall

23

Overhead Perspective

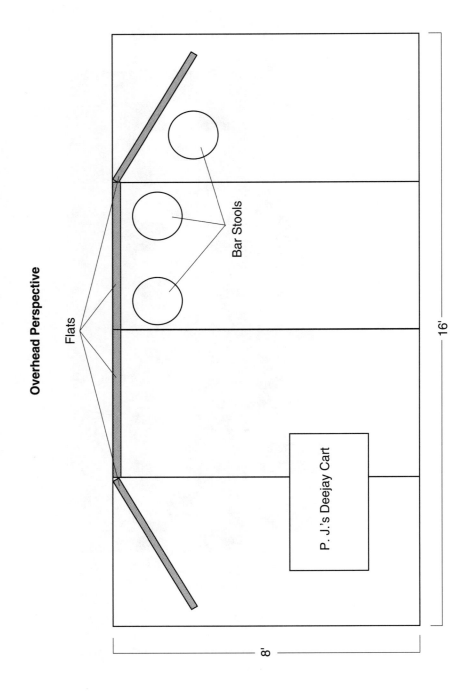

Flats

Bar Stools

P. J.'s Deejay Cart

16'

8'

Prop List

The following is a list of props needed for the primary action of the production. It does not include props that individual wait staff characters may choose to have for their performance.

General Onstage/Around Room

- Pay phone mounted on the wall or a phone on P. J.'s booth
- 3 to 5 stools
- "Bomb Shelter" sign on the ladies rest room door
- Various '50s-era prizes for raffle, such as Ovaltine, Spam, yo-yos, etc.

Scene 1

- Large quantity of straws
- Trick ketchup and mustard (optional)
- Fake stacked tray (optional)

Scene 2

No specific props designated

Scene 3

- Bingo cards
- Wrapped bubble gum (like Bazooka)

Scene 4

- Small birthday cake with candles
- Birthday hats
- Car keys

Scene 5

- Props specific to "This Was Your Life" game show

Scene 6

- Bingo tumbler with balls
- Bingo prize—Ovaltine, Spam, etc.

Scene 7

- "Lollipop"*—3 oversize lollipops made from Styrofoam disks and dowels with colored cellophane over them
- "Great Balls of Fire"*—squirt bottle for Flodene
- Burger Queen—checkered tablecloth "cape," spatula "scepter," and tiara with burger bun

- "Splish Splash"*—flotation devices, shower caps, scrub brushes, and bubble stuff

---

*Songs listed are suggestions only. Other songs may be used instead. See copyright page for important notice.

Uncle Phil's Diner

Scene 1

(As the guests are being seated, P. J. is up front playing recorded music. When most of the guests are in and seated, he begins Scene 1.)

P. J.: Hey, all you hair hoppers and big boppers, welcome to Uncle Phil's Diner where the food is fresh, and so is the help. I'm P. J. the deejay, and I'll be spinning the platters and serving up a tasty helping of licorice pizza. *(Holds up vinyl album)* I'll be bringing you all of today's hits, each one recorded in state-of-the-art high fidelity. (WAIT STAFF: "Ooooo!") Hey, let me take a minute to introduce our fine wait staff. Our head waitress, and a veritable institution here at Uncle Phil's, is Flodene.

FLODENE: Hey, P. J.! *(To guest)* You there, elbows off the table!

P. J.: She can take your order, correct your table manners, and yell for Phil in a single breath. And that's Hazel, Flodene's baby sister. She's the hostess with the mostest. How's it going over there, Hazel?

HAZEL: Not now, P. J. I'm kind of busy. *(To guest)* Hold your horses, buster. Everybody gets a seat.

P. J.: And over there is Central High's chess champion of the month, three years running—Wally!

WALLY (*to audience*): If anyone needs a chess tutor, I have some cards.

P. J.: It's no surprise that Wally is still looking for a date for the big dance, so watch out, ladies. Over there is Bunny Sue, head cheerleader at Evergreen High School.

BUNNY SUE: Evergreen! Evergreen! Rah! Rah! Rah!

CINDY LOU (*reacts to* BUNNY SUE *with disgust and starts her cheer*): Central High! Central High! Fight! Fight! Fight!

P. J.: And that's Bunny Sue's crosstown rival, Cindy Lou, head cheerleader at Central High. OK, girls, break it up. That young man over there is Ritchie. He's running for class president at Central High.

RITCHIE (*to audience*): Remember, a vote for Ritchie is a vote for me!

P. J.: That slogan needs a little work, buddy. And that lovely little lady in the prom dress is our own Tammy. Be sensitive tonight, folks. She's only here because her date stood her up for the prom. How are you doing over there, Tammy?

TAMMY: I'm fine, P. J. Thanks. (*To her table*) Does anyone have a tissue? (*She takes guest's napkin and cries into it.*)

P. J.: Hang in there, Tammy. Next is our little grease monkey, Tony.

TONY: Yo, P. J.!

P. J.: Tony works over at Bob's Garage during the day but moonlights here to make some extra money. Hey, Tony, did you wash your hands when you came in tonight?

TONY: Sure, P. J. (TONY *holds up black-stained hands, looks surprised; wipes them on his pants and holds them up again; is still surprised; runs to the kitchen.*)

P. J.: Don't worry, folks. We'll have him sanitized for your protection. That's Jimmy over there. He's just waiting tables until he gets discovered and hits it big as an actor.

JIMMY (*strikes "movie star" pose*): Hey, P. J.!

28

P. J.: Uncle Phil's resident beauty expert is the lovely LaVonna. She's only waiting tables to help pay off the damages after the (*P. J. and the rest of the* Wait Staff *all make finger air quotes as he says*) "unfortunate incident" at Mr. Fred's House of Beauty.

LaVonna: Well, the good news is, hair grows back—most of the time.

P. J.: Our all-star waiter over there is Johnny "The Rocket" Fultz. He's a shoo-in for all-state quarterback.

Johnny: Go, Lumberjacks!

P. J.: Just remember—*hand* people their food, Johnny. (Johnny *has a tray of food over his head as if he's about to throw it like a football. He hears* P. J., *remembers, and then hands it to the table.*) Our resident Boy Scout is Billy Mayfield.

Billy (*snaps to attention, salutes, and says very militarily*): Weblo Troop Number 1174 reporting for duty, sir!

P. J.: He's a little behind on his merit badges, folks, so don't be surprised if he helps you across the street to your car after dinner. Last, but not least, is little Gertrude Agnes Liggonberger.

Gertie: That's "Gertie" to my friends.

P. J.: She's a whiz with calculus, so if you need help figuring out your tip, call her over. (Gertie *pulls out a slide rule and waves it over her head.*)

Uncle Phil (*pokes his head through the kitchen door and yells to* P. J.): Hey, P. J., I'm paying you to play records, not gab with the guests. Is the band here yet?

P. J.: Not yet, Uncle Phil. They'll be here any minute. (*To audience*) Hey, everybody, that's my Uncle Phil. Say hi to the folks, Uncle Phil.

Uncle Phil: Hey, folks.

P. J. (*to audience*): Remember our staff is here to serve you. Staff, remember that? (Wait Staff *groans, "yeah, yeah, we remember," etc.*) So sit back and enjoy your meal, and the band should be here shortly.

SCENE 1 EXTRA BITS* (See "Individual Event Descriptions" for details.)
>   **Straws on table**
>   **Trick ketchup and mustard**
>   **Fake stacked tray**
>   **Raffle**

Scene 2

P. J.: Ladies and gentlemen, could I have your attention, please. I have a very important announcement to make. In keeping with government war defense regulations, Uncle Phil's Diner has just completed its bomb shelter! (WAIT STAFF *cheers.*) We do regret to announce that the warning siren hasn't been installed yet. (WAIT STAFF *groans "ahhh."*) However, in the meantime, we have developed our own civil defense warning. (WAIT STAFF *cheers.*) In case of a nuclear attack, this is what you'll hear. (TAMMY *has made her way to the stage and lets loose with the highest, longest, and loudest note she can hit.*) Remember, folks, this has only been a test. In the event of a real emergency, please proceed in an orderly fashion to the bomb shelter, which is located in the ladies' rest room, through the third stall on the right . . . or maybe it's the left. Oh well, back to some great music.

(UNCLE PHIL *has entered and come onstage during the siren. After the siren bit,* TONY *walks up and speaks to* UNCLE PHIL.)

TONY: Uncle Phil, I need to change my schedule from Thursdays to Fridays.

UNCLE PHIL (*a little frustrated, but listening*): Tony, this is a *job*, not a hobby. If I let everybody have the schedule they wanted, I'd end up only having waiters every other Tuesday under a full moon.

TONY: I know, I know. But this is really important.

UNCLE PHIL: OK, let's hear it.

TONY: I took your suggestion about helping others and volunteered to work one night a week serving dinner at the rescue mission downtown. They really need people on Thursdays, but I can see if they can use me another night.

UNCLE PHIL (*a little humbled*): That's OK, Tony. I'll change the schedule for you. I think it's really great of you to help out down there. (PHIL *gets an idea and says excitedly.*) Hey, I could send some extra meat loaf over with you.

~~TONY~~ *Pinky* (*nervously trying to avoid hurting* PHIL's *feelings, and spare the people at the rescue mission a helping of meat loaf*): Wow, Uncle Phil. That's really generous, but, uh . . . (*Looks around room nervously*) I think my order is up. Bye and thanks again. (*He runs away.*)

MOM (*having overheard the whole conversation, says proudly*): My, that ~~boy~~ *girl* has sure come a long way in the last couple of years. You were sure right about him, Phillip.

UNCLE PHIL: All some of these kids need is a chance.

(*Phone rings and* UNCLE PHIL *answers it.*)

UNCLE PHIL: Hello? Yes, this is Phil. Who is this? The De-who? The Desotos? Oh yeah, you're the band that is supposed to be here playing right now. Where are you guys? You're where? (*Give a landmark that the audience will recognize as very close to your facility.*) Oh, that's real close. We're right around the corner at the next signal. You can't miss us. And hurry. I have customers waiting. (*Hangs up phone. To* P. J.) This is your responsibility, you booked these guys. I know that kid, Jimmy Martin. He gets lost going to school at least twice a week. Well, nephew or no nephew, I told my sister I'd give you one more chance. You better come up with something to stall until they get here.

P. J.: OK, OK. I got just the thing.

PRODUCTION NUMBER (P. J. *plays a recorded song [song suggestion—"Hand Jive"]. As soon as the music starts, the* WAIT STAFF *drops what they are doing and runs to their places on the stage and around the room to perform. Some are very excited and into it, while others perform very grudgingly, but all of them appropriate to their character.*)

SCENE 2 EXTRA BITS*
   Cheerleaders get crowd yelling
   Raffle

Scene 3

(PHIL *and* P. J. *are onstage as phone rings again.*)

UNCLE PHIL: Hello? Yeah, this is Phil. You're where?! You're at (*give another landmark 15 to 20 minutes away*). How'd you get there? You went *left* at the signal? Why did you do that? When I said we were right around the corner, I meant *right* around the corner. (*Pause*) Well, turn around and come back the way you went. And hurry! (*Hangs up phone*)

MOM: What's the matter, Phillip?

UNCLE PHIL: Oh nothing, Mom. The band is late, and people are going to start leaving if we don't find something to keep them busy.

MOM: You know what people like? A nice friendly game of bingo.

UNCLE PHIL (*stares at* MOM *in disbelief; turns and yells toward audience*): FLODENE! (FLODENE *comes to the stage.*) Do something! (PHIL *leaves stage.*)

FLODENE: I don't know what to do. (*Searches her pockets and pulls out handfuls of bubble gum*) All I have is a bunch of bubble gum.

(P. J. *and* FLODENE *look at each other, pause for a moment and without speaking a word, get the same idea, turn to the crowd and start yelling simultaneously.*)

P. J.: We need some volunteers, who wants to play . . . (*Etc.*)

FLODENE: Who likes gum? Who wants some gum?

BUBBLE BLOWING CONTEST*

(*After the contest,* P. J. *plays another recorded song. After the song,* WALLY *and* JOHNNY *meet SR and talk while* GERTIE *and* BUNNY SUE *meet SL and talk. To help direct the attention up front,* WALLY *and* GERTIE *should be wearing wireless mikes. During this dialogue,* P. J. *should leave the stage.*)

32

WALLY (*to* JOHNNY): So, Johnny, how do you get the girls to talk to you?

JOHNNY: Well, it helps if you're the captain of the football team.

WALLY: I'm the captain of the chess team.

JOHNNY: It's not quite the same. Don't worry, there's someone special out there just for you.

GERTIE (*to* BUNNY SUE): I just know my Prince Charming is out there, Bunny Sue.

BUNNY SUE: Well, how will you know who he is?

GERTIE: I'll just know him when I see him.

(*As the song begins, the house lights go out.* BUNNY SUE *and* JOHNNY *freeze in place, as does the rest of the* WAIT STAFF *throughout the room, and two spotlights hit* GERTIE *and* WALLY. *Each has just noticed the other, and they begin to flirt across the room. They react accordingly to the words of the song.*)

NERDS IN LOVE*

(*While* WALLY'S *verse "plays in his head,"* GERTIE *is acting shy and embarrassed but flattered because she knows he is looking at her. When he sings about her grace, she should do something awkward. When he sings about the ketchup on her face, she should touch her face and then notice that there is ketchup on it and wipe it off. In general, she acts like a young girl trying to get the attention of a guy.*)

WALLY: I've just seen an angel
   Standing by table number 5.
   I've never felt so confused; I've never felt so alive.
   I'm in love with her beauty,
   I'm in love with her grace,
   I'm even in love with that ketchup on her face.
   Could she be the one?
   Is this love at last?
   Is there anything finer, than finding love at the diner?

   Could she be the one?
   Will this love be true?

33

Is it my imagination, or is it just desperation?
Could she, would she be the one for me?

(While GERTIE's *verse* "plays in her head," WALLY *tries to impress her by acting "manly." He should take* JOHNNY's *football and bobble it clumsily when she sings about the football star. When she says, "famous movie star," he yells in his best Jerry Lewis voice, "Hey, Lady!" He should, in general, be awkward and goofy as he tries to impress her.*)

GERTIE: Who is that angel
  Watching from afar?
  Is he some football hero
  Or some famous movie star?

WALLY: Hey, Lady!

GERTIE: I can tell that he's healthy,
  I can tell that he's smart,
  Because he keeps his milk money so close to his heart.

  Could he be the one?
  Is this love at last?
  What if he's just a loser?
  Well, beggars can't be choosers.

  Could he be the one?
  Will this love be true?
  Would it be so alarming, if he was my Prince Charming?
  Could he, would he be the one for me?

(As the instrumental portion of the song plays, WALLY *and* GERTIE *rush toward each other but miss and pass each other. They take off their glasses, wipe them on something, put them back on, rush at each other again, and finally meet. They do a very silly, corny mock-ballet including exaggerated lifts, turns, and jumps during the last chorus.*)

WALLY: Could she be the one?

GERTIE (*echoes*): Could he be the one?

WALLY: Will this love be true?

GERTIE (*echoes*): Will this love be true?

BOTH: Is it my imagination, or is it just desperation?

GERTIE: Could he be the one?

WALLY (echoes): Could she be the one?

GERTIE: Is this love at last?

WALLY (echoes): Is this love at last?

BOTH: Is there anything finer, than finding love at the diner?

WALLY: Could she

GERTIE: Would he

BOTH: Be, the one for me?

(During the last few words, they part and drift back to their starting positions. As the song ends, the lights come up and they both pick up their conversations with JOHNNY and BUNNY SUE as they walk away. The rest of the WAIT STAFF also comes alive again and picks up exactly where they left off. The entire song was a dream and never really happened except for the audience.)

---

*Sheet music included in Production Pack MPK-825. Call 1-800-877-0700 to order.

Scene 4

(UNCLE PHIL is onstage and JOHNNY walks by him.)

UNCLE PHIL: Hey, Johnny. Did your dad get that delivery job?

JOHNNY: Yeah, they gave him the job, but he's going to have to turn it down because our car is broken and we can't afford to fix it.

UNCLE PHIL (thinking a moment, reaches into his pocket and pulls out a set of keys): You know, we're done with all our pickups by 7 A.M. every morning, and our truck just sits there for the rest of the day. Your dad is welcome to use it anytime after that.

JOHNNY (very surprised): Really? Are you sure, Uncle Phil?

UNCLE PHIL (*hands him the keys*): Yeah, I'm sure.

JOHNNY: Thanks.

UNCLE PHIL: If there's anything else I can do, let me know. And say hi to your family for me.

(*P. J. is at his station. The phone rings. P. J. answers it and calls for UN-CLE PHIL. PHIL comes from the kitchen and takes the phone. He is not looking forward to it.*)

UNCLE PHIL: You're where? You're in (*give a city name about a half hour away*)! I told you to turn around and go back the way you came. (*Pause*) What do you mean, you're still looking for a place to turn around? Just do it!

MOM (*overhearing*): Phillip, now would be a good time for bingo.

UNCLE PHIL: P. J.! Do something!

P. J. (*nervously*): Don't worry, Uncle Phil. I'll think of something. (*Gets an idea*) I know, let's serve dessert!

(WAIT STAFF *cheers. After most of the dessert is served, P. J. announces someone's birthday.*)

BIG HAPPY BIRTHDAY PRODUCTION*

SCENE 4 EXTRA BITS
2nd all-cast production number (song suggestion—"Shake Your Tail Feather")

Scene 5

(*Phone rings. PHIL answers.*)

UNCLE PHIL: Yeah. You're where? What do you mean you don't know? Didn't you turn around like I told you? Good. Well, what do you see around you? (*Gives another landmark that is 30 to 45 minutes away.*) How did you get there? Oh, never mind, just get back in the car and head east. And hurry up!

MOM (*sweetly, waving bingo cards*): Oh, Phillip!

UNCLE PHIL (*avoids giving MOM an answer, yells to P. J.*): P. J.!

P. J.: I'm way ahead of you, Uncle Phil. Don't worry, I got it taken care of. (*Game show theme song plays as P. J. begins "This Was Your Life."*)

THIS WAS YOUR LIFE GAME SHOW (*P. J. should have the opening announcement handy and can read it off the page, but should put the character introductions on 3" x 5" cards. The opening game show music starts and P. J., in his most "Game Show Announcer" voice, starts.*)

P. J.: Ladies and gentlemen, it's time for America's favorite game show, "This Was Your Life"! The show that brings back people from your yesteryears to celebrate your present-day life achievements . . . it's a real blast from the past. Let's learn a little bit about today's special guest . . . He was born just outside of Bakersfield (*any town will do*) to proud parents, Beauford and Wilma (*insert last name here*). He was shaped and molded in this community by many people throughout his childhood, but especially by the people at Bakersfield High School . . . home of the Bakersfield Badgers. He was president of the "cheeses of the world club" and founder of the Better Treatment for School Mascots Association. After high school he went on to make millions and millions of dollars as the inventor of that little red stringy thing on the top of a gum wrapper. Let's give a big welcome to (*insert name here*). (*P. J. has the contestant sit on a stool or chair.*) You must be very excited to be here. We've flown in some very special people from your past to celebrate your life! Here is how it works. You're going to hear a voice from your past from offstage and you'll try to guess who it might be. Ready? OK, let's see if you recognize this voice . . .

MRS. WINKLESTEIN (*from offstage; she mispronounces the contestant's name slightly—for example "Timmy" instead of "Tommy," thinking he was a different kid*): Oh, I just love my little (*incorrect name*). He always brought the hall pass back when he went to the rest room.

P. J.: That's right. It's your elementary school kindergarten teacher! Let's give a warm welcome to Mrs. Winklestein!

MRS. WINKLESTEIN (*approaches and pinches his cheeks*): Oh, it's so good to see you little (*incorrect name*).

P. J.: Mrs. Winklestein, tell us a little bit about *(correct name)*.

Mrs. Winklestein: Oh my little *(incorrect name)*. He went the entire kindergarten year without eating **one** crayon. He's such a sweet boy. He always had an apple for me on Fridays. I just love my little *(incorrect name)*.

P. J.: Mrs. Winklestein, excuse me, but his name is *(correct name)*, not *(incorrect name)*.

Mrs. Winklestein *(pauses and runs the real name through her head out loud, realizing she's been thinking about the wrong kid. She eventually realizes who **this** kid really was, a real troublemaker, screams the real name out loud, and then lunges for the contestant. She has to be restrained by P. J., who then calls for a big male* Wait Staff *member to carry her offstage over his shoulder. The whole time she is screaming at the contestant)*: I remember you. That was the worst year of my life. *(Etc.)*

P. J.: Apparently you're not who she thought you were. Well, let's meet our next guest. Do you recognize this voice?

Mrs. Lavoris *(from offstage)*: That's a good boy. Now rinse and spit!

P. J.: That's right! It's your childhood dental assistant, Mrs. Lavoris. Welcome her to the stage, everyone.

Mrs. Lavoris: Hi there, *(name)*. It's been a long time since we've seen you for a checkup. I remember when *(name)* lost his first little toothie, and when his first big molar came in. And who can forget the time you chipped your tooth on Uncle Phil's meat loaf?

Uncle Phil *(from somewhere out in the room, yells)*: HEY!

Mrs. Lavoris: You needed a root canal . . . that was the year we added the pool. Well, let's see how you're doing . . . (P. J. *and another* Wait Staff *member tip him back in his chair while* Mrs. Lavoris *puts on a rubber glove and proceeds to check out his gums.)* It looks like you've been practicing good dental health. Now you get to choose a prize from the goodie basket. *(She holds up a basket with candy or small prizes and he takes one.)* See you in six months. Good-bye.

P. J.: Are you ready for our next guest? Do you recognize this voice?

COACH FARBER *(from offstage)*: Drop and give me 20, butterfingers!

P. J.: That's right, it's the pride of the Bakersfield High Badgers, Coach Farber! How are you doing, Coach? (COACH FARBER *enters and makes his way to the stage. This is not a happy man. He obviously has a grudge against this former player.*)

COACH FARBER *(sarcastically)*: Oh, just great!

P. J.: Certainly, you must remember this guy.

COACH FARBER *(grumbling)*: Oh yeah, I remember him. In fact, I think about him every day as I go to my crummy little office at that crummy little high school that I've been working at for 20 years. *(To contestant)* Do you know why I've been stuck at that school? Because of you, butterfingers! Remember the "big game" *(name)*? Five seconds to go, we're down by 4 on the three-yard line . . . is it coming back to you? Olsen hikes it to Sedgewick, Sedgewick fades back to throw, looks for who's open. Do you remember who was open *(name)*? That's right, *it was you!* Wide open in the end zone. All by yourself. You could have been having a picnic in there. Remember what happened then? Sedgewick tosses the ball right into your hands, and you actually caught it! But you got so excited about catching it, you dropped it and we lost the game. Bye-bye, state championship. Bye-bye, Coach Farber's future in the college and professional leagues. Drop and give me 20, *(name)!* *(If guest is willing to do it, let him or her.)* Just what I thought! You still don't have it!

P. J.: Well, this isn't going as well as we planned, but let's see if you recognize this voice from your past.

CHRISTINE *(from offstage)*: I know that you only went to the prom with me because your dad works for my dad's company, and he needed a promotion, but I knew from the moment we met that we were meant to be together forever.

P. J.: Let's welcome your senior high school prom date . . . Christine Cunningham. (CHRISTINE *enters in her old prom dress with a wilted corsage. She has naively been waiting for the contestant to call her, not realizing he never will.*)

CHRISTINE: Hi, (name). It's great to see you again. Remember after our magical prom date, you said you would call? Well, I've been waiting by the phone.

P. J.: You've been waiting a long time, Christine.

CHRISTINE (very promptly): Seven years, five months, 13 days, and (looks at watch) three hours. I thought maybe your phone was broken, but when I was going through your trash, I found your phone bill and everything's in order . . . by the way, congratulations on your new job, and I love what you've done with the house. I see it every night when I drive by to see you. I know we're still meant to be together. See, I still have the prom corsage . . .

P. J. (calls for TONY PETRELLI to come get her offstage): Tony, we might have a security problem.

CHRISTINE (TONY starts to escort her off): Wait! Wait! We were meant to be together forever . . . forever . . . (She looks at TONY as he drags her offstage.) Hi, what's your name?

TONY: Tony Petrelli.

CHRISTINE: That's my favorite name . . . Tony. Tony Petrelli. Christine Petrelli. Mr. and Mrs. Tony and Christine Petrelli. (TONY runs offstage with her chasing him.)

P. J.: Looks like finally she's over you . . . well, it's time for our last guest. Let's see if you recognize this voice?

SGT. O'CONNEL (from offstage): You have the right to remain silent!

P. J.: That's right. It's your parole officer, Sgt. O'Connel!

SGT. O'CONNEL (comes in wearing police uniform): We've been looking for you for a long time. (Puts handcuffs on him) Let's go. We're taking you downtown. (He escorts him offstage and out of sight so he can return to his seat afterward.)

P. J.: Well, it looks like we won't be seeing (name) again for at least 5 to 10. That's the end of our show. Join us next time for . . . "This Was Your Life"! (Game show music plays out.)

SCENE 5 EXTRA IMPROV BITS*
Raffle

Scene 6

(PHIL, P. J., and MOM are onstage as phone rings again. They let it ring a LONG time before PHIL finally shuffles over, head hanging low, and answers it.)

UNCLE PHIL: Yeah. Uh-huh. Uh-huh. Uh-huh. *(PHIL hangs up phone, looks at P. J. With a deadpan expression says the name of a city an hour and a half away.)* *(Name of city.)* *(PHIL looks at MOM, who still has her cards ready, says with false excitement.)* I have a great idea. Let's play bingo!

BINGO GAME*

Scene 7

(Phone rings. PHIL enters from the kitchen.)

UNCLE PHIL: I'll get it! Hello. You're where? You're at *(name of known restaurant, or "Golden Arches" in a town two hours away)*. *(Giving up)* Yeah, that's the place. Just come on in and set up wherever you want. OK, see you soon. *(Hangs up)* Well, at least someone will hear some live music tonight. P. J., Flodene, get up here. Well, the band is a no-show. What are we gonna do? We promised these people live music.

FLODENE: Well, unless you want to drag out your accordion, we're stuck.

UNCLE PHIL *(pointing at the instruments next to the stage)*: Whose instruments are those?

P. J.: They belong to the guys in the kitchen. Remember, you told them they could practice here after hours when they were done cleaning up.

UNCLE PHIL: Are they any good?

FLODENE: They sound pretty good when I'm running the vacuum.

41

UNCLE PHIL: Well, get 'em out here. I'll take anybody at this point.

FLODENE (*yells into kitchen*): All right boys, here's your big chance. Get out here and entertain these folks.

(*The kitchen guys enter from kitchen wearing aprons, paper hats, hair nets, gloves, etc. They pick up their instruments and play an instrumental number.*)

Song No. 1 (*Song suggestion—"At the Hop."* You can have a couple come up and jitterbug on the stage to this song.*)

FLODENE: We've got the band, now we just need some singers.

WALLY: Flodene, I'd like to sing. I'm really good. I once . . .

FLODENE (*interrupting him*): Wally, what I really need right now is a cleanup over on table 7. Those people are slobs. Thanks, hon. Now who can I get? I know, Bunny Sue, Cindy Lou, Gertie. Get up here girls. We need your voices. (*They come on stage and* FLODENE *places* BUNNY SUE *at the mike and gives* GERTIE *and* CINDY LOU *a big lollipop. She has one extra lollipop.*) I need one more girl here. Hazel, honey. Can you come and give us a hand up here?

HAZEL (*very adamant about not wanting to perform*): No way, sis. You're not getting me up there

FLODENE (*goes and gets her, shoves her on stage, gives her the lollipop, arguing with her the whole time*): You'll do it and you'll like it. We all need to pitch in and help. (*Etc.*)

Song No. 2 (*Song suggestion—"Lollipop."* Band plays "Lollipop."* BUNNY SUE *sings lead and the three girls sing backup and do choreographed backup moves.* GERTIE *and* CINDY LOU *are into it and having a ball, especially* GERTIE. HAZEL *does it very grudgingly, and* FLODENE *has to keep stepping in to correct her and put her where she belongs.*) (NOTE: BUNNY SUE *and* CINDY LOU *can be replaced by any other two female* WAIT STAFF.)

FLODENE: Well, let's see. Who else can we get up here?

WALLY: Flodene, I was wondering if I could sing a . . .

FLODENE (*cuts him off, gets rid of him*): Wally, the trash needs to be emptied, hon. Thanks.

WALLY (*frustrated*): OK, Flodene.

FLODENE: P. J.! I know *you* can sing.

P. J. (*embarrassed*): Well, not really.

FLODENE (*laying on the guilt*): I know your mother sacrificed to pay for several years of voice lessons, and she would be very disappointed in you if she were to find out you refused to sing when you know . . .

P. J. (*dropping false modesty and giving in*): OK, OK. You win. I do have one little number I've been working on. (*Turns around, flips up his collar, turns back around, the epitome of cool*)

Song No. 3 (*Song suggestion—"Great Balls of Fire."* * After a couple of lines of his singing, the female* WAIT STAFF *runs to the front screaming like crazy bobby-soxers.* FLODENE, *the guardian of all that is decent, is embarrassed by their behavior and tries to shoo them away by spritzing them with her spray bottle of water. She finally figures, "If you can't beat 'em, join 'em!" So she does.*)

FLODENE (*fanning herself, obviously overwhelmed by P. J.'s performance*): See, I knew you could sing. Your mother would be proud. That was money well spent. OK, who's next? Let me see?

WALLY: Flodene, I'd like to . . .

FLODENE (*cutting him off again*): Wally, can you refill the saltshakers on table 5?

WALLY: Sure, Flodene. But I really can . . .

FLODENE (*cuts him off*): Thanks, hon. OK, let's bring up Tammy. She has the voice of a nightingale, that girl. Come on up, Tammy.

Song No. 4 (*Song suggestion—"Tammy."* * TAMMY *comes up onstage and sings her sad love song. At the end, she cries and runs from the room.* P. J. *and* FLODENE *are concerned. They have a brief conversation and then ask for the crowd's help.*)

43

P. J.: You know, folks, Tammy has been a little down since being stood up for the prom. We've decided to do something to cheer her up. We're going to crown her Uncle Phil's Burger Queen, so when she comes back in the room, let's all give her a royal welcome.

(TAMMY *enters, royal song plays. She is led to stage while crowd cheers. Onstage she is given a tablecloth cape, a spatula scepter, and a tiara with a hamburger bun attached to it.*)

P. J.: Tammy, you may not be the prom queen, but you're officially the Uncle Phil's Burger Queen for 1956, with all the rights and privileges that go with it, including first pick of any of the day-old pies for half price.

(TAMMY *beams. She leaves waving to the crowd.*)

FLODENE (*dabbing her eyes, very touched*): That was beautiful. Now we need something peppy. Here at Uncle Phil's we specialize in good clean fun. (*To band*) Why don't you boys play that cute little number you do while you're washing the dishes.

Song No. 5 (*Song suggestion—"Splish Splash."* * *Band members or male* WAIT STAFF *member can sing lead. When the second verse starts, the other male* WAIT STAFF *enter wearing various flotation devices, shower caps, and carrying scrub brushes while blowing bubbles around the room. The other* WAIT STAFF *can also blow bubbles.*)

FLODENE: That was great, boys. Thanks. Well, I think that's everyone that I know of who can sing, so I guess it's time to say goodni . . .

WALLY (*interrupting*): OK, Flodene. I cleaned up table 7, no easy feat, by the way, I emptied the trash and filled the saltshakers on table 5. *Now* will you let me sing?

FLODENE: Why didn't you tell me you could sing, Wally?

WALLY (*aghast*): But I've been trying to tell you that I can sing for the last half hour.

FLODENE: Oh, is that what you were trying to tell me? Well, are you any good?

WALLY: Am I any good? (*Proudly*) When I was in the Herbert Hoover Junior High School 1952 Cavalcade of Talent, the Herbert Hoover Junior High School *Gazette* said of my performance (WALLY *pulls a folded up newspaper article out of his pocket, unfolds it and reads*), "Wallace Klinghopper's rendition of the George and Ira Gershwin classic 'Summertime' was enjoyed by all." Did you hear that? It said "enjoyed by *all.*"

FLODENE (*sarcastically*): Very impressive. But I don't think this is really a Gershwin kind of crowd, Wally.

WALLY: Sure they are. (*To audience*) You folks would love to hear some Gershwin, wouldn't you? (*He gets them cheering.*) See, I told you so. (*To band*) Do you guys know "Summertime"? (*Band nods and says, "Oh yeah, sure we do," etc. They nod knowingly at each other and begin to play a strong rock and roll classic.*)

Song No. 6 (*Song suggestion—*"JOHNNY BE GOOD."*)

WALLY (*recognizing that this is not Gershwin*): Guys, I don't think that's Gershwin. It's kind of fast. Are you sure you know what song I was talking about? (*He finally starts singing very tentatively. As the song goes along and he gets more comfortable, he begins to move a little and get into it more and more, never quite achieving "cool," but almost.*)

---

*Songs listed are suggestions only. Other songs may be used instead. See copyright page for important notice.

Scene 8

FLODENE: Wow, Wally. You were right. This crowd does love Gershwin. (PHIL *joins them onstage.*) Well, Phil, I think that's all we're going to get out of these guys tonight.

UNCLE PHIL: Oh well, it was better than a grease fire in the kitchen.

(*Loud crash offstage in kitchen.* TONY *peeks his head out the door.*)

TONY: Sorry, Uncle Phil. I'll clean it up.

FLODENE: You know, Phil, sometimes I wonder why you keep hiring these kids. It seems like they cost you more money than they make for you.

PHIL: Well, Flodene, sometimes they do. But the truth is, they remind me a lot of me when I was their age. You know, I wasn't always the warm and friendly guy I am today. (FLODENE *rolls her eyes.*) I was actually kind of a rough kid, unsure of what I was going to do with my life. I was used to fighting for what I wanted and didn't know any other way. I had a hard time getting a job because people took one look at me and didn't want to take a chance. Until one godly man, who owned a diner just like this one, took that chance. He brought me in, taught me the business, and showed me a different way to live. And when I messed up, he let me know it, but he never stopped believing in me. He taught me about grace. Because of him I was able to get in the navy and make something of myself. That's why I'm committed to always having room in my diner for kids like these to work.

(Loud crash offstage in kitchen. WALLY *peeks his head out of the door.)*

WALLY: Sorry, Uncle Phil. I'll clean it up.

UNCLE PHIL: And I have to trust that the Lord is going to honor that and keep them from putting me out of business. Well, everyone, thanks for coming tonight. If you've enjoyed our service tonight half as much as we've enjoyed serving you, then, uh, we've enjoyed ourselves twice as much as you have. Wait a minute, that can't be right. Well, anyway, come back again soon to Uncle Phil's Diner—where the food is fresh and so is the help!

Appendixes

Time Line

First half hour—guests arrive and are seated

Second half hour—food is served and eaten

Scene 1—Begins soon after guests arrive
- Wait Staff characters introduced by deejay as they are serving.
- Improv with each other and guests.
- Straws on table bit.
- Trick ketchup and mustard.
- Fake stacked tray.

Scene 2
- Uncle Phil welcomes guests, gets first call from the band.
- Air raid siren.
- Deejay plays production number song—Wait Staff performs.
- Cheerleaders get crowd yelling.

Scene 3
- Second phone call; band is farther away.
- Mom wants bingo.
- Bubble gum blowing contest.
- "Nerds in Love"* duet.

---

*Sheet music included in Production Pack MPK-825. Call 1-800-877-0700 or visit a local Christian bookstore to order.

Scene 4
- Third phone call; band is even farther away.
- Uncle Phil tells deejay to play more music.
- Mom asks about bingo again. No!
- Dessert and coffee are served while music is played.
- BIG Happy Birthday production.
- Deejay plays production number song—Wait Staff performs.

Scene 5
- Fourth phone call, band is farther away.
- Mom asks about bingo.
- Deejay does "This Was Your Life."

Scene 6
- Fifth phone call; band is farther away.
- Finally, bingo! (See page 63 for **Bingo Call** order.)

Scene 7
- Final phone call; no band coming.
- Phil asks Flodene about band instruments.
- Kitchen guys set up and play.
- Various wait staff perform.
- Tammy is "Burger Queen."

Scene 8
- Uncle Phil thanks everyone for coming.
- Message dialogue with Flodene.
- Band plays out.

Back-up Time Fillers—in case of extra time you can fill it up with a few other bits.
- Raffles
- Hula hoop contest

Individual Event Descriptions

Scene 1

• **Wait Staff characters introduced by deejay as they are serving.** P. J. the deejay welcomes everyone, introduces each Cast A member and gives guests some funny information about them from character bios.

• **Straws on table bit.** A table near the front and center is selected ahead of time to be the "straw" table. Their wait person doesn't give them any straws for their drinks. If they ask for them, great. If not, the wait person realizes the mistake and yells across the room, "I need some straws on Table 5." P. J. picks up on it and announces it over the speakers. For the next several minutes, every wait staff person will make a point of passing by this table and tossing a handful of straws onto it, oblivious to the fact that there is already a mound of them.

• **Trick ketchup and mustard.** You can buy these at a joke store. They are plastic ketchup and mustard dispensers that have colored string in them. When you squeeze them it looks like it is shooting out the ketchup and mustard. These can be carried around by a couple of people, like Wally, and accidentally squirted at guests.

• **Fake stacked tray.** This consists of a plastic serving tray, or a plastic tub, and lots of plastic dishes. The dishes need to have a hole drilled in them and a string put through them and attached to the tray so they appear to be stacked a few feet high and are very unstable. This can be carried through the dining room a few times.

Scene 2

• **Air raid siren.** Playing into the '50s theme, P. J. gives a brief update on Phil's bomb shelter preparation. Unfortunately, he hasn't had his siren installed yet, so in case of an attack, they have prepared an early warning system—Tammy. Tammy comes up on stage and hits the biggest, highest, and longest note she can.

• **Production number** (song suggestion—"Hand Jive"*). This is a production number that all of Cast A (except Phil and Mom) participate in. Cast B can also learn it if they want to. P. J. will play the song and everyone, no matter what he or she is doing, will stop, run to his or her spot on the stage or in the room and do this number. It needs to be choreographed and look rehearsed. Each person should do it as their character would. For example, some of the guys won't be good at it, the cheerleaders are perfect, the nerds are clumsy, etc.

- **Cheerleaders get crowd yelling.** The two cheerleaders from rival schools have tables next to each other in the middle of the room. They are constantly competing with each other. They eventually get their halves of the room chanting, "We've Got Spirit, Yes We Do . . ." until Uncle Phil breaks it up.

Scene 3

- **Bubble gum blowing contest.** Three to five members of the audience are brought up on stage and each is given the same number of pieces of bubble gum. The goal is to see who can open them up, chew them, and blow a big bubble the fastest. Can be done more than once.

- **"Nerds in Love" duet.** (Sheet music is included in Production Pack MPK-825; call 1-800-877-0700 to order.) See script for dialogue. This is a dream sequence. It is done by Wally and Gertie who had been lamenting their love lives to their friends. They spot each other from across the room, the lights dim, two spotlights hit them, and the song begins. It is as if they are thinking it, not singing. They go into a humorous ballet number and when the song finishes, the lights come back up and they both wander away as if it never happened.

Scene 4

- **BIG Happy Birthday production.** A guest, hopefully a good sport, is pulled from the audience and led to the stage in a big fanfare. He or she is given a crown and a cake with candles as the wait staff and audience sing "Happy Birthday."* During the song, P. J. leans over as if the person is telling him something. He stops the song and announces that it is *not* the person's birthday. It is as if a balloon is popped. Everyone slumps in disappointment, as if this person has lied to them. Someone blows out the candles, takes the cake, removes the crown, and everyone walks away leaving the person alone on the stage. (See NOTE on selecting audience participants.)

- **Production number** (song suggestion—"Shake Your Tail Feather"*). Another choreographed number for Cast A. This song shows a lot of the moves from the '50s, like the monkey, the swim, the watusi, and so forth.

Scene 5

• **Deejay does "This Was Your Life."** Member of audience, another good sport, is brought up on stage and challenged to "remember" voices and people from the past which really isn't his or hers. Various members of the wait staff play these people, or if you can, it would be better to use people from Cast B or a different group altogether. (See NOTE on selecting audience participants.) The script for this is written about a man and works better if he is over 40.

Scene 6

• **Finally Bingo!** This is a "rigged" game. The wait staff hands out cards and pencils to everyone. Mom shows off the valuable prize— a can of Spam. She gets up front with her bingo tumbler (can be bought at a toy store) and calls out numbers. She can make lots of funny remarks about rowdiness, chatting, and so forth. She can use funny, '50s-era words with each ball—for example, "B-15. That's Bomb shelter 15." After several balls are pulled out, everyone in the room gets "bingo" at the same time. Mom doesn't know what to do. She holds up her one prize, drops it, and runs. See page 63 for **Bingo Call** order.

Scene 7

• **Final phone call.** No band is coming. Kitchen guys set up and play. They can begin with an instrumental like "At the Hop."* If you want, have a couple people get up and perform the jitterbug, and so forth, onstage.

• **Various wait staff perform.** Flodene drags different wait staff onstage and makes them sing. Some totally reluctantly, some comic, some good/hammy. Songs suggested are "At the Hop"* by the band, "Lollipop"* sung by a lead and three backups who have big suckers they perform with. One of the backups can be tough girl, Hazel, who is not into it at all and another can be Gertie who is totally into it and having the time of her life. "Great Balls of Fire"* can be sung by P. J. The girls come running up to the stage screaming and fawning over him. "Tammy"* is sung by Tammy, who was stood up that night by her prom date and came into work in her dress. "Splish, Splash"* can be sung by a male waiter or band member. The other guy waiters come out in inner tubes and shower caps blowing bubbles around the room. Finally, Wally, the nerd, wants to sing "Summertime"* by Gershwin, but instead, the band launches into a rock classic such as "Johnny Be Good."* When he can't stop them, he starts singing timidly, but soon is belting away.

● **Tammy is "Burger Queen."** After Tammy's song "Tammy,"* she leaves dejected and sad. To cheer her up, P. J. gets everyone to cheer when she walks back in. They lead her to the stage and crown her "Burger Queen," complete with spatula scepter, tablecloth cape, and burger bun tiara.

---

*Songs listed here are merely suggestions. Other songs can be used just as easily. See copyright page for important notice.

Scene 8

● **Message dialogue with Flodene**

● **Band plays out**

BACKUP TIME FILLER

● **Raffle.** This can take place at several different times during the evening. If you plan to do this, everyone needs to be given a ticket upon entrance to the event and then throughout the evening P. J. and Flodene have a raffle. It is fun to do and gives everyone in the room the chance to play something. The prizes should be something funny and '50s era like Spam, Ovaltine, yo-yos, and so forth.

● **Hula Hoop contest.** This would work the same way as the bubble gum contest. You can bring three to five people onstage and time them to see who can spin the hula hoop the longest.

Cast Descriptions

Uncle Phil: diner owner/cook

> Character age range: Plays as 40 to 60.
>
> Character type: Think of Ed Asner or Vic Taybeck.
>
> Twenty years cooking in the navy taught Phil a thing or two. That's why "Uncle Phil's" has such an extensive menu. (Ha, Ha!) Nobody sports an apron like Uncle Phil, or grease stains. He runs the diner with an iron spatula. Well, he thinks he runs the place . . . but between Mom, P. J., and Flodene's "help," he has his hands full.
>
> Most likely to be heard saying:
> "FLODENE!"
> "Not now, Mama!"
> "These burgers aren't getting any hotter!"
> "Did anyone here try the meat loaf?"
>
> Costume suggestion: Greasy apron over a white shirt. Paper hat. Could have a fake "Navy" or "Mom" tattoo.

Mom

> Character age range: Plays as at least 20 years older than Phil.
>
> Character type: A crazy hybrid of "Aunt Bea" and "Mama" (Vicki Lawrence).
>
> Uncle Phil's doting mother. She was quite a gal back in her day. Midwest Polka Queen of 1930-33. Mom loves to "suggest" things to Phil. Her hearing challenge and cane don't seem to hold Mom back. She's always right in the thick of the action . . . well, between naps, that is.
>
> Most likely to be heard saying:
> "You like bingo, don't you?"
> "How's the food tonight? I love it, but the doctor won't let me eat it anymore."
> "Phillip, did I already take my medicine?"
> "Play a little bingo. It will relax you."
>
> Costume suggestion: Old lady clothes and wig (if needed). Shawl and cane.

P. J. the deejay

> Character age range: Plays as a high school senior.
>
> Character type: Game show host/'50s deejay.

The abbreviation is for "Phil Jr." P. J. is Uncle Phil's nephew and is designated a "junior" to distinguish between them. His mother twisted Phil's arm to get him a job at the diner. P. J. is a kind of game show host, lounge lizard, and bad wedding deejay all rolled into one. But also a very nice kid. He is the one who hired the band and since they haven't shown up, there is some tension between him and his uncle throughout the night. P. J. is the emcee for the evening. In addition to playing songs, he keeps the guests entertained by staging various contests, raffles, and games. He even belts out a song when the band plays. Always smooth, never flustered, P. J. is the guy you want in charge of your next party.

Most likely to be heard saying:

"Here's a dedication going out to that special girl at table number 7 . . . from Wally!"

"Here's a dedication going out to that special girl at table number 5 . . . from Wally!"

Flodene: the head waitress

Character age range: Plays as 35 to 45.

Character type: Think of the original "Flo" from "Mel's Diner."

What would Phil do without Flodene? She's undoubtedly the queen of all diner waitresses. Wisecracking, New Jersey born, Flodene takes pride in serving her customers. "Does your mother know you eat with those hands?" Flo is multitalented. She can take your order, correct your table manners, and yell for Phil in a single breath. The younger waitresses revere Flodene as the epitome of waitresses. They perspire to be just like her!

Most likely to be heard saying:

"You saving that ketchup on your face for later?"

"Finish that burger, there are starving people in this world, you know."

"Hey, are you single? My sister is a really good speller."

"Let me see those hands, mister. Go wash these right now." (Sends guest to washroom and checks his hands when he comes back.)

Costume suggestion: Waitress-looking uniform with an apron across the front. Cat's-eye glasses with chain around the back. Kerchief in her pocket and name tag. Gaudy.

Hazel: the hostess

Character age range: Plays as late 20s.

Character type: A tough cookie with an attitude.

Flodene's "baby" sister and hostess extraordinaire. She'll tell you where to go—sit that is. Hazel considers herself a fashion maven and with little or no prompting she'll give you her opinion about your apparel. Hazel reads all the movie mags, so she knows what's hip and what's not. Flodene is just so proud of baby Hazel. Much to Hazel's chagrin, Flo is always embarrassing her baby sister by bringing up her great success as the fifth grade spelling bee champion. "Spell something for the people, Hazel!"

Most likely to be heard saying:

"Hold your horses, everybody gets a seat."

"You know, you should really wear pearls with that sweater."

"James Dean would never wear a tie."

"I can't believe you're wearing white shoes . . . it's *after* Labor Day, you know."

Costume suggestion: Bowling shirt and jeans. Scarf around her neck and glasses.

Wally

Character age range: Plays as a high school senior.

Character type: The classic "nerd."

Wally is the classic stereotype of the nerd. His pants are too short, his shirt is too tight, his pocket is full of pencils and pens, and his glasses have tape in the middle of them. He can be a little forgetful, so he keeps his milk money in an envelope pinned to his shirt pocket, labeled of course. Wally is the reigning chess champion at his school and in the top of his class academically. But he'd trade it all for a date. He is a little lacking in the social graces and doesn't quite know how to ask out girls. He tries all night and receives a variety of interesting excuses. Eventually, Wally proves he can be just as "cool" as the other kids.

Most likely to be heard saying:

"Hi, Mr. Kroeger. Remember me from science class? Sorry again for blowing up the lab."

"Do you have a date for the big dance yet?" (Asks waitresses, not guests.)

"I was going to try out for the football team, but practice would interfere with my clarinet lessons, so my mom said I couldn't."

Costume suggestion: Short pants and white short-sleeved shirt. Thick black glasses with tape in the middle and a pocket protector full of pens and pencils. Small envelope with some change in it, marked "milk money" pinned to his shirt.

Gertie

Character age range: Plays as a high school senior.

Character type: The ultimate female braniac nerd.

Or Gertrude Agnes Liggonberger to her friends. Gertie is a bit more than socially challenged. Her affinity for calculus and Greek history does not attract the fellows. But Gertie is an optimist; she just knows her Prince Charming is out there. He might even work at Uncle Phil's. Maybe tonight is the night. Maybe tonight she'll finally get a date.

Most likely to be heard saying:

"How do you meet boys?"

"Do you think Wally is cute?"

"Maybe I shouldn't wear my glasses."

"Is that your date? How did you get him to go out with you?"

Costume suggestion: Frumpy sweater and skirt. Thick glasses. Various medals and awards can be pinned to the sweater.

Tammy: the prom queen

Character age range: Plays as a high school senior.

Character type: The classic prissy prom queen with *big* hair.

Meet poor, pitiable Tammy. All dressed up and nowhere to go! She's a prom queen who missed her own prom. Never fear, P. J. and Flodene come to the rescue. They hatch the plan to crown Tammy the Burger Queen of Uncle Phil's, complete with a hamburger crown and burger flipping scepter. There's not a dry eye in the room as Tammy promenades as queen.

Most likely to be heard saying:

"I would just like to thank . . ." (Reciting her would-be acceptance speech.)

"Maybe he's just lost. I'll just wait a little longer."

"Are you here on a date? That must be nice." (Cries)

"Do you like my dress? I made it myself." (Cries)

Costume suggestion: '50s-looking prom dress with a wilted corsage. *Big* hair.

Bunny Sue

Character age range: Plays as a high school senior.

Character type: Think of a perennial pepster

Head cheerleader at Evergreen High School, Bunny Sue fancies herself the loudest, most peppy cheerleader in town. Everything is a cheer for Bunny Sue. She can't speak to you without turning the conversation into a cheer. Hence, her unusual waitress style. "OK! Hit it! Give me your order! Give it to me now. Give me your order. Or you won't get your chow. Yeah! Yeah!"

Most likely to be heard saying:

Turns guests' names into a cheer. She's very proud of this ability.

"Do you think I'm a better cheerleader than Cindy Lou?"

"Hey, everybody, let's cheer for our table."

Costume suggestion: Actual cheerleader outfit that could pass as '50s. The biggest difference is that the skirts then went to the knee. Be careful of year numbers on outfit. NOTE: You can change the names of the high school in the play to match these outfits.

Cindy Lou

Character age range: Plays as a high school senior.

Character type: A do-or-die cheerleader.

Head cheerleader at Central High School and arch-nemesis to Bunny Sue and her squad. Cindy Lou has not recovered from the humiliation suffered at the hands of Bunny Sue at the last crosstown rival game. This causes a bit of trouble since both pepsters work at Uncle Phil's. It's happened on many occasions, that the two cheer queens have forgotten where they are . . . and lead their customers in an all-out frenzied cheer war. "We've got spirit. Yes, we do! We've got spirit. How about you?" And so on . . . and so . . . and so on . . .

Most likely to be heard saying:

"Winning is not everything; it's the only thing."

"I can jump higher than her any day of the week."

Makes up cheers about everyone's dinner

Costume suggestions: Same as Bunny Sue, but from a different high school.

LaVonna: the beautician

Character age range: Plays as mid 20s to early 30s.

Character type: Think beauty school dropout.

LaVonna is an aspiring (more like perspiring) beautician to the stars. Try though she may, LaVonna has had a bit of trouble graduating from the 13 beauty schools she has attended. Lucky for LaVonna there's always Uncle Phil's where her cousin Flodene holds a job open for her. Good thing—she hasn't paid off all the damages since that unfortunate little mishap at Mr. Fred's House of Beauty. LaVonna lives by her motto, "Hair grows back." The only problem is, LaVonna can't seem to stay out of people's hair, literally! Watch out—if LaVonna says she wants to tease you, it's no joke. Have comb will travel.

Most likely to be heard saying:

"Oh boy, split ends. Let me just trim them up a bit."

"You know, you would make a great redhead."

"The secret to a really great beehive is teasing, teasing, teasing."

"You should really wrap toilet paper around your head at night."

She can actually put rollers, rubber bands, and so forth, into guests' hair.

Costume suggestion: Skirt and blouse with white lab coat over them. The lab coat can have the "Mr. Fred's" logo on it and could be a little singed and have some burn holes in it from the "unfortunate incident." She should have *big* hair and lots of makeup. She can carry a bag with hair and beauty supplies in it to "practice" on her customers.

Ritchie

Character age range: Plays as a high school senior.

Character type: Clean-cut, all-American boy.

No last name for Ritchie. That's because he's running for class president and one name is easier to remember at the polls. Ritchie is working the crowd for votes all night long. He's constantly talking about his numerous political platforms such as "bringing back macaroni and cheese with little smokies to the hot lunch menu." He carries with him plenty of "Vote for Ritchie" paraphernalia like buttons and flyers with his picture on them. He might even cruise through some of the musical numbers with a big "Vote for Ritchie" sign.

Most likely to be heard saying:

"Remember, a vote for Ritchie is a vote for me."

"How do you feel about this macaroni and cheese issue?"

"What would it take for me to get your vote?"

Costume suggestion: Very neat and clean-cut. Slacks with a cardigan sweater over a white button-down shirt. He can wear his campaign buttons as well as other kinds of voting buttons and ribbons.

Tony Petrelli

Character age range: Plays as a high school senior.

Character type: Grease monkey; Brooklyn accent.

Tony comes straight from his job as a car mechanic every day to work at Uncle Phil's waiting tables. The only problem is he doesn't bother to clean up much. He is still wearing his stained coveralls, complete with ragged red towel and a bottle of window cleaner (water). Out of habit, he asks customers if their windshields need a good squeegee and then cleans their eyeglasses. Ketchup bottles can be checked with a dipstick (craft stick or coffee stirrer) and "checking under the hood" means lifting up the burger bun to see if everything is on it. He will probably discuss his customers' cars with them and offer his services.

Most likely to be heard saying:

"What'chu drivin'? Oh yeah, I saw you drive in. I think you need some brake work."

"Waiting tables is a lot like fixing cars. I get dirty doing both."

"Can I give your windshield a squeegee?"

Costume suggestion: Blue coveralls or jeans and a blue work shirt.

Jimmy Knight

Character age range: Plays as a high school student.

Character type: Surfer/actor.

Jimmy is just waiting tables until he's discovered and makes it big as an actor in Hollywood. Since acting is his life, he's always going to have two or three drama scenes with him at all times and he's going to need some of the customers to help him practice his lines. He may even make them do it over again "with feeling." He occasionally brags about his commercials for such products as Super Green's Rash Ointment or his brief stint as a crash test dummy for a car safety announcement.

Most likely to be heard saying:

"Can you practice this scene with me? I have an audition next week."

"Can you try that again with a little more feeling? I didn't really buy it."

"Who do you think I look more like: James Dean or Marlon Brando?"

Costume suggestion: He can either be in a Hawaiian shirt and jeans or some sort of costume as if he's just come from a rehearsal.

Johnny "The Rocket" Fultz

Character age range: Plays as a high school senior.

Character type: Your classic football jock.

This guy is the star quarterback for the football team, captain of the basketball team, varsity baseball, and so forth. You name it, he's got a letter on his jacket for it. He always carries a football with him and may even toss it around with Tony to show off his great hands. It's possible he might even place his trophy on the table while he's waiting on guests. He often tells story after story to the customers about his game-winning touchdown in the last three seconds of the championship game where the team was down by five and . . .

Most likely to be heard saying:

"Did I tell you about the time I won the championship game . . . ?"

"Who ordered the cheeseburger? OK, go long!"

Costume suggestion: Letterman jacket covered with pins. Be careful of year numbers.

Billy Mayfield

Character age range: Plays as a high school senior.

Character type: Clean-cut, Boy Scout type.

Billy is your dyed-in-the-wool Boy Scout. At least he hopes to be. Right now he is the city's oldest Weblo because he's a little behind in his merit badges. In order to become an actual Boy Scout he has to get signed off on several more items. So throughout the evening he will be asking his various customers to sign him off as he completes different tasks such as his origami badge for folding a guest's napkin into something. Another badge might be for patriotism, which he'll earn by singing the national anthem in a public place. He might also tell you about the time he was lost in the wilderness and made a compass out of match sticks and a can of Spam to point his way. Or the time he used his Swiss army knife to ward off a grizzly bear by tweezing his eyebrows.

Most likely to be heard saying:

"Will you help me sign off on a badge project?"

"Did I tell you about the time I was lost in the forest . . . ?"

Costume suggestion: This one could take some work. He needs a Boy Scout uniform that will fit an adult with a variety of patches on it. He can carry his Swiss army knife and a canteen that he can use to refill water glasses. He will need some specific tasks to get signed off on and some kind of form for people to sign when he has completed them.

Character backgrounds for THIS WAS YOUR LIFE cast:

Mrs. Winklestein: Older, sweet, and kindly-looking retired kindergarten teacher. Best if played by an older actress. She is as sweet as apple pie until she finds out she's thinking about the wrong little boy. Then she turns ugly. She should be 70ish looking with a print dress, glasses, shawl.

Mrs. Lavoris: Very medical and methodical about everything. Costume should be a nurse's outfit complete with old style nurse's hat. She needs a rubber glove, possible dental mirror, and a basket of "goodies."

Coach Farber: He's not in the best shape and a little crusty. He's a grumpy, middle-aged guy. Costume would be sweats with the top stuffed for a good out-of-shape gut, a baseball cap too! He should look in his 50s and can be played by an older actor.

Christine Cunningham: Ever since their prom date, which was a setup, she hasn't stopped thinking about the contestant and how they were meant to be. She's a little obsessed with him, to say the least. Costume should be the prom dress she wore that night complete with the same corsage. Of course, over the years the flowers have become wilted and her dress a little stained. She is more naive than crazy. She should *not* come off as a psycho stalker, but as misguided.

Sgt. O'Connel: A police outfit is a must. He doesn't say much but is great for a big finish. Police uniforms have not changed too much, so you can get away with a modern one. The hat can add a period look if you can find one.

Bingo Calls

Call numbers in this order. Bold numbers are winning numbers. Bingo card sheets are included in the Production Pack (MPK-825; call 1-800-877-0700 to order). Copy the cards onto card stock or heavy paper that is brown or white for best results. Try to hand the cards out in such a way that each table gets all eight different cards with as few repeats as possible.

- B-10
- **N-37**
- I-17
- **B-3**
- I-21
- G-47
- **G-51**
- N-39
- O-70
- N-33
- **O-64**
- B-9
- **I-24**

PERFORMANCE LICENSING AGREEMENT

**Lillenas Publishing Resources
Performance Licensing
P.O. Box 419527, Kansas City, MO 64141**

Name _____

Organization _____

Address _____

City _____ State ___ Zip _____

Play title: **UNCLE PHIL'S DINER** by Avanzino, Fisher, and Wilson

Number of performances intended _____

Approximate dates _____

Amount remitted* $_____

Mail to Lillenas at the address above.

Order your Production Pack (MPK-825) for this script from your local bookstore or directly from the publisher at 1-800-877-0700.

   *$35.00 for the first performance; $25.00 for each subsequent performance. Payable U.S. funds.

Please feel free to photocopy this page.

GL 450-100-391